for GCSE

Practice for book H1 part A

PATHFINDER EDITION

Contents

2	*Manipulation*	3
3	*The tangent function*	6
4	*Indices*	9
	Mixed questions	14
5	*Distributions and averages*	15
6	*Changing the subject*	18
7	*Increase and decrease*	22
	Mixed questions 2	27
8	*Sine and cosine*	28
9	*Using area and volume*	31
10	*Large and little*	35
11	*Gradients and equations*	41
	Mixed questions 3	47

PUBLISHED BY THE PRESS SYNDICATE OF THE UNIVERSITY OF CAMBRIDGE
The Pitt Building, Trumpington Street, Cambridge, United Kingdom

CAMBRIDGE UNIVERSITY PRESS
The Edinburgh Building, Cambridge CB2 2RU, UK
40 West 20th Street, New York, NY 10011-4211, USA
10 Stamford Road, Oakleigh, VIC 3166, Australia
Ruiz de Alarcón 13, 28014 Madrid, Spain
Dock House, The Waterfront, Cape Town 8001, South Africa

http://www.cambridge.org

© School Mathematics Project 2001
First published 2001

Printed in Italy by Rotolito Lombarda
Typeface Minion   *System* QuarkXPress®

A catalogue record for this book is available from the British Library

ISBN 0 521 01267 8   paperback

NOTICE TO TEACHERS
It is illegal to reproduce any part of this work in material form (including photocopying and electronic storage) except under
the following circumstances:
(i) where you are abiding by a licence granted to your school or institution by the Copyright Licensing Agency;
(ii) where no such licence exists, or where you wish to exceed the terms of a licence, and you have gained the written permission of Cambridge University Press;
(iii) where you are allowed to reproduce without permission under the provisions of Chapter 3 of the Copyright, Designs and Patents Act 1988.

2 Manipulation

Sections A and B

1. Write each expression without brackets and collect any like terms.
   (a) $7p - (3p + 7)$
   (b) $20 - (2k + 9)$
   (c) $5 - (n + 7)$
   (d) $6y - (5 - y)$
   (e) $4h - (7h - 1)$
   (f) $b - (5b - 3)$

2. For each expression, multiply out the brackets and collect any like terms.
   (a) $4p + 3(p - 2)$
   (b) $2h + 5(1 - h)$
   (c) $20 - 7(k + 2)$
   (d) $3n - 2(n - 7)$
   (e) $^-5(x + 1) + 9$
   (f) $6m - 5(3 - 2m)$

3. Simplify each of these expressions.
   (a) $3x^2 + 6x + 4x^2$
   (b) $8p + 5 + 4p^2 - 5p$
   (c) $4n^2 + 3n - 5n + 3$
   (d) $2r^2 + 16 - 3r^2$
   (e) $s^2 - 3s + s^2$
   (f) $h^2 - 6h + 3 + h$
   (g) $5y^2 + 6y - 2y^2 - 6 - y$
   (h) $8k^2 - 4k + 6 - 2k^2 + 3k$

4. For each expression, multiply out the brackets and collect any like terms.
   (a) $4p + p(p - 5)$
   (b) $h^2 + 4(1 - 3h)$
   (c) $2k^2 - k(k + 3)$
   (d) $2n - n(n - 9)$
   (e) $2x^2 - 2x(x - 2)$
   (f) $6m - 2m(3 - m)$

5. Write an expression for the area of the shaded shape in each of these.
   Simplify each expression by collecting any like terms.

   (a)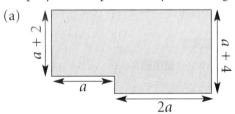
   (b)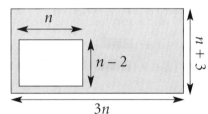

6. For each expression, multiply out the brackets and simplify
   (a) $p(p + 2) + 2(p + 3)$
   (b) $a(a - 1) + 3(a - 2)$
   (c) $2a(a + 3) + a(a - 2)$
   (d) $2x(x + 1) - 2(x + 4)$
   (e) $3y(y + 2) - y(6 - y)$
   (f) $4b(b - 3) + b(2b - 5)$
   (g) $3h(h + 5) - 2(h + 5)$
   (h) $4q(q - 1) - 2q(5 - q)$

7. Copy and complete each of these statements.
   (a) $a(a + 2) + \blacksquare(a + 2) = a^2 + 5a + \blacksquare$
   (b) $\blacksquare(p - 2) + p(p + 4) = p^2 + 6p - \blacksquare$
   (c) $\blacksquare(x + 3) + \blacksquare(x + 3) = x^2 + 6x + 9$
   (d) $2b(b + 2) + \blacksquare(b - 2) = 3b^2 + \blacksquare b$

Sections C and D

1 Multiply out the brackets and simplify each of these
   (a) $(x+2)(x+4)$
   (b) $(x+8)(x+1)$
   (c) $(x+11)^2$
   (d) $(x+3)(x-6)$
   (e) $(x-2)(x+9)$
   (f) $(x-9)(x+2)$
   (g) $(x-4)(x-5)$
   (h) $(x-7)(x-3)$
   (i) $(x-3)^2$

2 Find pairs of expression from the bubble that multiply to give
   (a) $a^2 + 5a + 6$
   (b) $a^2 - 5a + 6$
   (c) $a^2 + a - 6$
   (d) $a^2 - a - 6$
   (e) $a^2 - 7a + 12$
   (f) $a^2 - 8a + 12$
   (g) $a^2 - 9$
   (h) $a^2 - 16$

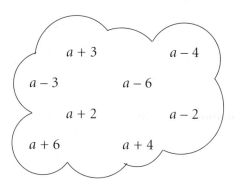

$a+3$, $a-4$, $a-3$, $a-6$, $a+2$, $a-2$, $a+6$, $a+4$

3 Find expressions for the unknown sides in these rectangles.

(a)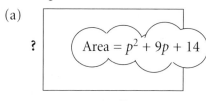

? ; Area = $p^2 + 9p + 14$; $p+7$

(b)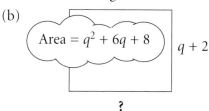

Area = $q^2 + 6q + 8$; $q+2$; ?

4 Copy and complete these identities
   (a) $(s+4)(\blacksquare\blacksquare\blacksquare) = s^2 - s - 20$
   (b) $(\blacksquare\blacksquare\blacksquare)(t-4) = t^2 - 6t + 8$
   (c) $(x+4)(\blacksquare\blacksquare\blacksquare) = x^2 + \blacksquare x + 24$
   (d) $(y-1)(\blacksquare\blacksquare\blacksquare) = y^2 - 10y + \blacksquare$

Section E

1 (a) Copy and complete the first three lines of this pattern.

$5 \times 6 - 1 \times 10 =$
$6 \times 7 - 2 \times 11 =$
$7 \times 8 - 3 \times 12 =$
.
.
.
$\blacksquare \times \blacksquare - n \times \blacksquare =$

(b) Write an expression for the nth line and simplify it. What does this prove about the results for this pattern?

2 Make up a pattern of your own where every line gives a result of 4.

3 A $2 \times 4 - 1 \times 3 =$
      $3 \times 5 - 2 \times 4 =$
      $4 \times 6 - 3 \times 5 =$
      $\vdots$

   B $3 \times 4 - 1 \times 4 =$
      $4 \times 5 - 2 \times 5 =$
      $5 \times 6 - 3 \times 6 =$
      $\vdots$

   C $2 \times 6 - 1 \times 7 =$
      $3 \times 7 - 2 \times 8 =$
      $4 \times 8 - 3 \times 9 =$
      $\vdots$

(a) For each of these patterns write an expression for the nth line and simplify it.

(b) For which of these patterns will the result always be:

   (i) the same   (ii) an even number   (iii) an odd number

Section F

1 This grid of numbers has ten columns. A diamond outlines some numbers.

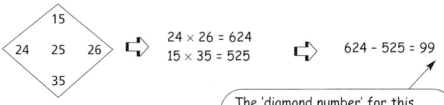

Sam calculates the 'diamond number' like this
   • Multiply the opposite corners and find the difference between the results.

$24 \times 26 = 624$
$15 \times 35 = 525$

$624 - 525 = 99$

The 'diamond number' for this diamond is **99**.

   • This is the 'diamond number'.

(a) Sam labelled the top number of a diamond as n.
    Write an expression for each number in the diamond.

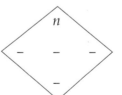

(b) Write an expression for the 'diamond number' on this grid.
    What does this tell you about 'diamond numbers' on this grid?

2 What would the 'diamond number' be on a grid with 8 columns?

3 The tangent function

Section A

1 Find the opposite sides in these triangles.

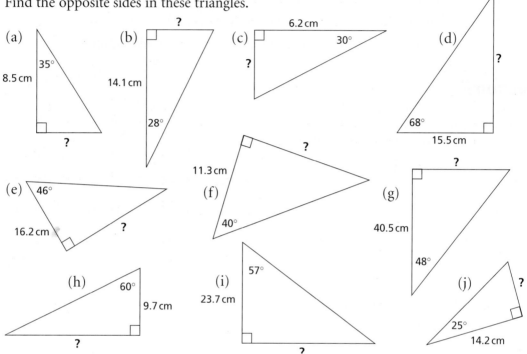

Section B

1 Find the adjacent sides in these right angled triangles.

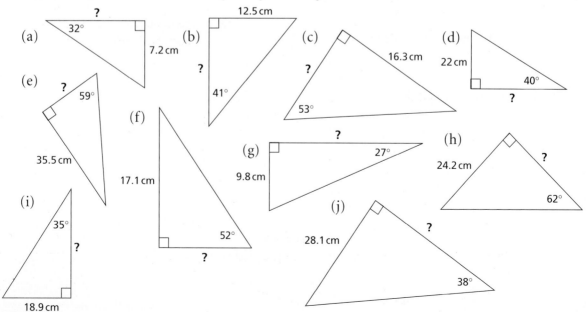

2 Find the missing sides. Some are opposite and some are adjacent.

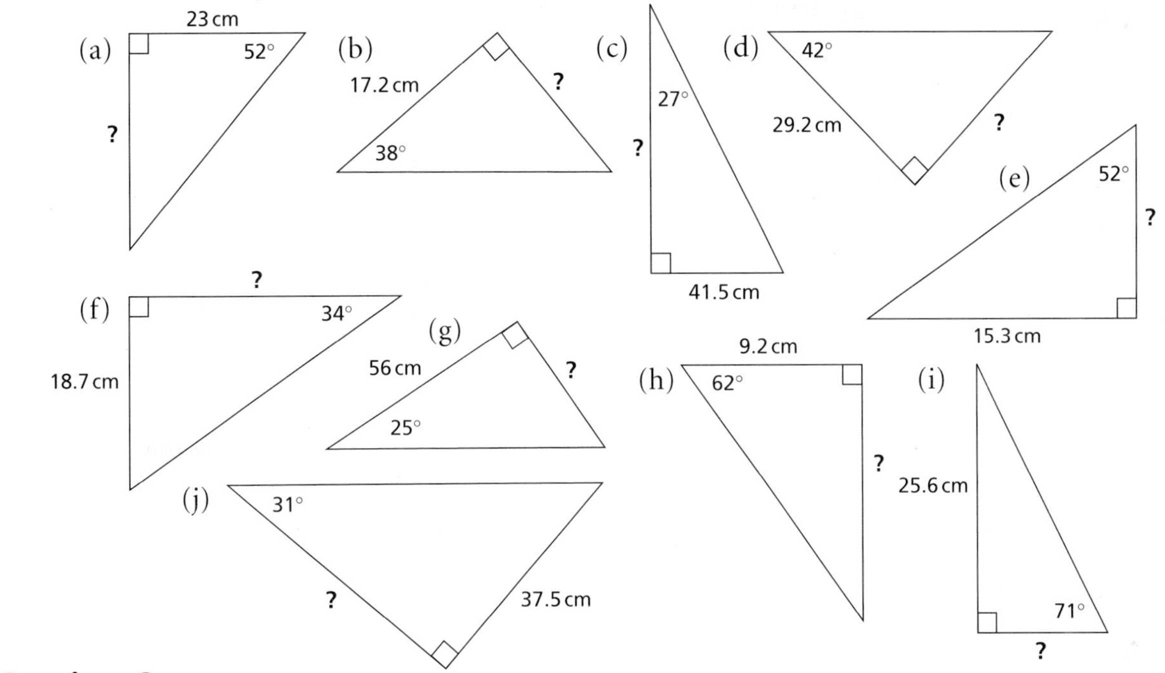

(a) 23 cm, 52°, ?

(b) 17.2 cm, 38°, ?

(c) 27°, ?, 41.5 cm

(d) 42°, 29.2 cm, ?

(e) 52°, ?, 15.3 cm

(f) 34°, ?, 18.7 cm

(g) 56 cm, 25°, ?

(h) 9.2 cm, 62°, ?

(i) 25.6 cm, 71°, ?

(j) 31°, ?, 37.5 cm

Section C

1 Find the angle in each triangle.

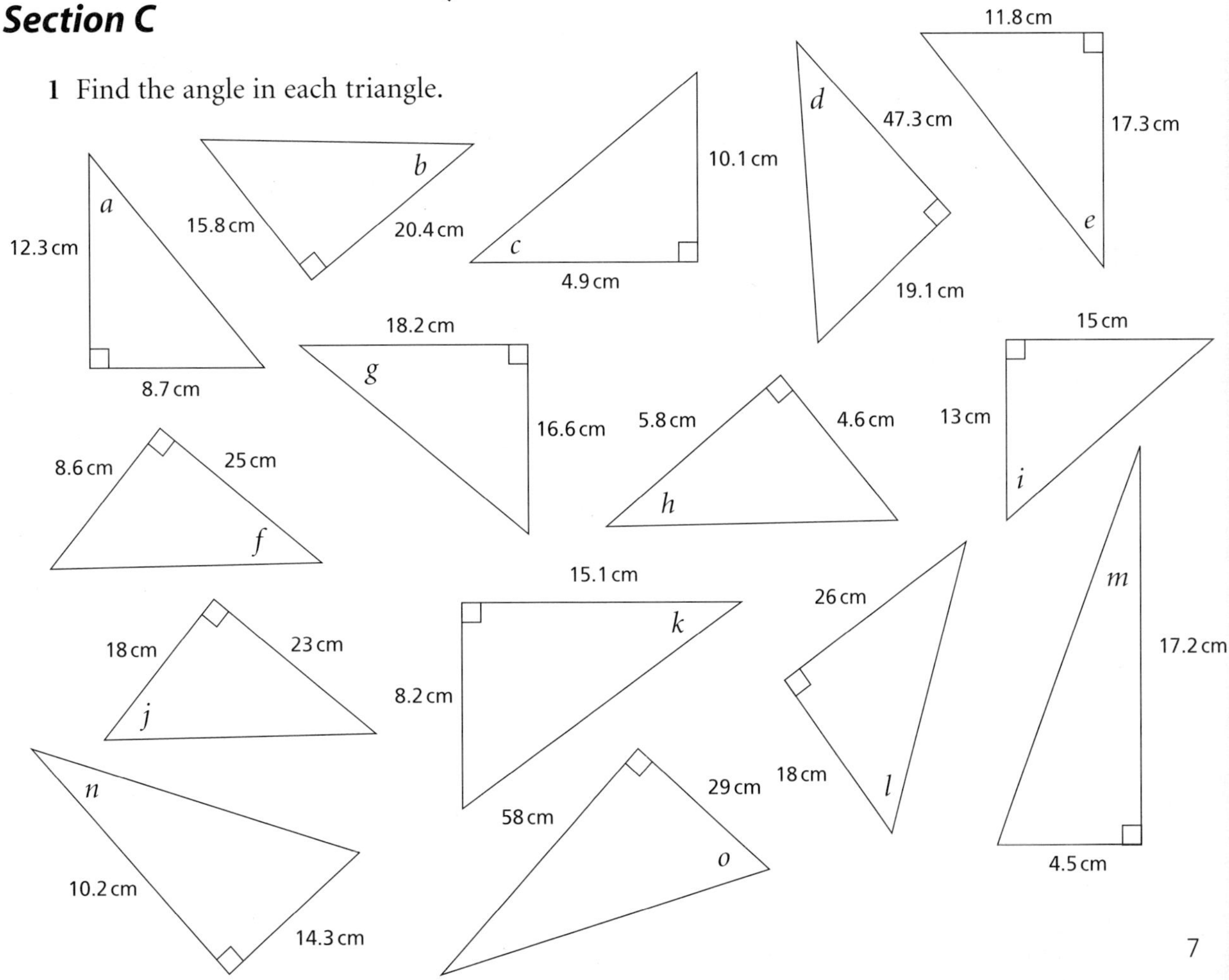

a: 12.3 cm, 8.7 cm

b: 15.8 cm, 20.4 cm

c: 10.1 cm, 4.9 cm

d: 47.3 cm, 19.1 cm

e: 11.8 cm, 17.3 cm

f: 8.6 cm, 25 cm

g: 18.2 cm, 16.6 cm

h: 5.8 cm, 4.6 cm

i: 15 cm, 13 cm

j: 18 cm, 23 cm

k: 15.1 cm, 8.2 cm

l: 26 cm, 18 cm

m: 17.2 cm, 4.5 cm

n: 10.2 cm, 14.3 cm

o: 58 cm, 29 cm

7

Section D

1. Calculate the length of the base of this ridge tent.

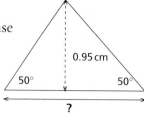

2. The coordinates of the vertices of triangle ABC are A(2, 5), B(6, 12) C(6, 5). Find angle CAB.

3. A tower is 21 m high.
   Point R is 45 m from the base of the tower.
   Calculate the angle of elevation from point R.

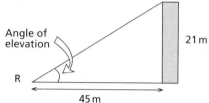

4. Zara walks from A, 9 km east to B and then 4 km south. Find the bearing of C from A.

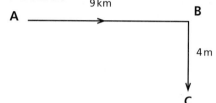

5. ABC is an isosceles triangle. Find the area of the triangle.

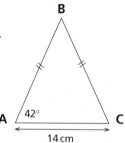

4 Indices

Section A

Answer questions 1 to 6 without using a calculator.

1. Write these using index notation
   (a) $2 \times 2 \times 2 \times 2$
   (b) $10 \times 10 \times 10$
   (c) $7 \times 7 \times 7 \times 7 \times 7$

2. Calculate the value of:
   (a) 2^6
   (b) 5^3
   (c) 10^4
   (d) 20^3

3. Calculate the value of:
   (a) $12 + 3^2$
   (b) $5^3 - 10^2$
   (c) 7×5^2
   (d) $5^3 \times 2^3$

4. Which is bigger:
   (a) 2^{10} or 10^2
   (b) 5^4 or 4^5?

5. A piece of paper is folded in half so that it is 2 sheets thick.
   It is folded in half again so that it is 4 sheets thick.
   It is folded in half three more times.
   (a) How many sheets thick is it now?
   (b) Write your answer using index notation.

6. In diagram 1 there are 3 'ends' identified by 'blobs'.
   In diagram 2 there are 9 'ends'.

   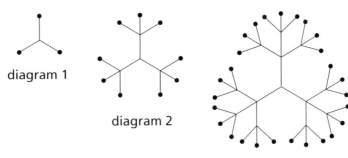

   diagram 1

   diagram 2

   diagram 3

   (a) How many ends are there in diagram 3?
   (b) If you continued drawing the pattern, how many 'ends' would there be in diagram 5?
   (c) Write down the number of ends in diagram 12 using index notation.
   (d) Write down an expression for the number of ends in diagram 'n'.

7 Arrange each set of numbers in order of size starting with the smallest.
   (a) 6^9 8^8 10^7 12^6 14^5 (b) 2^{11} 3^7 5^5 7^4

8 Solve the following equations.
   (a) $x^5 = 59049$ (b) $8^x = 4096$ (c) $x^8 = 5764801$

9 There is an error in the end digit of each of these calculations.

   Explain without using a calculator why each calculation cannot possibly be correct.

   (a) $2^{21} = 2097153$
   (b) $5^8 = 390623$
   (c) $4^8 = 65530$
   (d) $6^{10} = 60466174$

10 The date 3 April 2081 can be written as 3/4/81.
   This date is unusual as $3^4 = 81$.
   2 March 2008 can be written as 2/3/08 and it is true that $2^3 = 8$.
   Find at least four dates d/m/y like this in the 21st century so that $d^m = y$?

Section B

1 Find the prime factorisation of each of these numbers and write it using index notation.
   (a) 80   (b) 441   (c) 72   (d) 600

2 200 can be written as: $2^x \times 5^y$
   Find x and y

3 49 000 can be written as $2^r \times 5^s \times 7^t$
   Find r, s and t.

4 $207 = 3^2 \times 2^3$
   Use this prime factorisation to find all six factors of 207

5 Use prime factorisation to find the LCM's of the following:
   (a) 15 and 24   (b) 18 and 40   (c) 36 and 108   (d) 24, 30 and 80

6 Use prime factorisation to find the HCF's of the following:
   (a) 40 and 108   (b) 36 and 80   (c) 96 and 180   (d) 420 and 560

7 A packet of sweets can be shared equally between 2 or 3 or 4 or 5 people.
   What is the smallest number of sweets that could be in the packet?

8 A cuboid 144 mm long, 126 mm wide and 108 mm tall is cut up into cubes all the same size.
   (a) If there is no waste, what are the dimensions of the largest possible cube?
   (b) How many of these cubes will there be?

Section C

1. Find the numbers missing from.
   (a) $5^3 \times 5^2 = (5 \times 5 \times 5) \times (5 \times 5) = 5^\blacksquare$
   (b) $\dfrac{10^5}{10^4} = \dfrac{10 \times 10 \times 10 \times 10 \times 10}{10 \times 10 \times 10 \times 10} = 10^\blacksquare$
   (c) $4^4 \times 4^3 = (4 \times 4 \times 4 \times 4) \times (4 \times 4 \times 4) = 4^\blacksquare$
   (d) $\dfrac{3^5}{3^2} = \dfrac{3 \times 3 \times 3 \times 3 \times 3}{3 \times 3} = 3^\blacksquare$

2. Match each calculation with an answer.

Calculation
(a) $7^4 \times 7^6$
(b) $7^{20} \div 7^8$
(c) $7^3 \times 7^3 \times 7^3$
(d) $(7^8 \times 7^9) \div 7^2$

Answer
A: 7^9
B: 7^{10}
C: 7^{15}
D: 7^{12}

3. Find the value of ■ in the following calculations
   (a) $2^3 \times 2^\blacksquare = 2^{12}$
   (b) $10^6 \div 10^\blacksquare = 10^3$
   (c) $a^\blacksquare \times a^5 = a^{20}$
   (d) $\dfrac{c^\blacksquare \times c^3}{c^4} = c^8$
   (e) $\dfrac{7^5 \times 7^4}{7^\blacksquare} = 7^3$

4. Copy and complete these multiplication grids.
   (a)
×		2^3	
2^9	2^8		
	2^{10}		
2^8			2^{10}

   (b)
×	b^4		
		b^{11}	b^{14}
b^7			b^{13}
	b^9		

5. Find the value of x and y in each statement.
   (a) $2^3 \times 3^2 \times 2^4 = 2^x \times 3^y$
   (b) $5^3 \times 3^2 \times 5^4 \times 3^6 = 5^x \times 3^y$
   (c) $\dfrac{4^9 \times 3^6}{4^3 \times 3^4} = 4^x \times 3^y$
   (d) $\dfrac{3^6 \times 5^9 \times 3^7}{5^4 \times 3^5 \times 5^3} = 3^x \times 5^y$

6. Find the value of n in each statement.
   (a) $(3^4)^2 = 3^4 \times 3^4 = 3^n$
   (b) $(7^3)^4 = 7^3 \times 7^3 \times 7^3 \times 7^3 = 7^n$
   (c) $(5^3)^4 = 5^n$
   (d) $(a^5)^3 = a^n$

7. Find the value of x.
   (a) $(3^2)^x = 3^8$
   (b) $(2^x)^3 = 2^9$
   (c) $(5^3)^2 = 5^x$

8. Copy and complete.
   (a) $9^4 = (3^2)^4 = 3^\blacksquare$
   (b) $8^5 = (2^\blacksquare)^5 = 2^\blacksquare$
   (c) $81^3 = (3^\blacksquare)^3 = 3^\blacksquare$
   (d) $125^2 = 5^\blacksquare$
   (e) $64^3 = 4^\blacksquare$
   (f) $27^5 = 3^\blacksquare$

9 Find four pairs of equivalent expressions

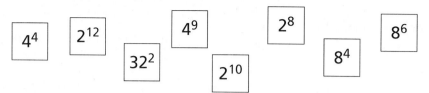

Section D

1 Simplify:
 (a) $3x^2 \times 5x^3$
 (b) $3y^2 \times y^5$
 (c) $2w \times 3w^2 \times 6w^3$
 (d) $(3y^2)^4$
 (e) $(2u^5)^3$
 (f) $(v^2w^3)^5$

2 Simplify:
 (a) $\dfrac{10x^5}{2x^3}$
 (b) $\dfrac{8y^2}{16y^5}$
 (c) $\dfrac{12v^4}{3v}$
 (d) $\left(\dfrac{6x}{18x^3}\right)^2$
 (e) $\left(\dfrac{8w^5}{4w^3}\right)^3$
 (f) $\dfrac{8x^3 \times 3y^2}{6x^2 \times 4y^3}$

3 Copy and complete these multiplication grids

(a)
×		x^3	
$2x$	$4x^3$		
		$4x^6$	
$3x^2$			$9x^7$

(b)
×			$2y^3$
$5y$			
$2y^3$		$4y^7$	
	$3y^4$		$2y^5$

Section E

1 What is the value of 5^0?

2 Copy and complete:
 (a) $\dfrac{1}{4} = \dfrac{1}{2^\blacksquare} = 2^\blacksquare$
 (b) $\dfrac{1}{27} = \dfrac{1}{3^\blacksquare} = 3^\blacksquare$
 (c) $\dfrac{1}{64} = 4^\blacksquare$
 (d) $\dfrac{1}{1000} = 10^\blacksquare$
 (e) $5^{-3} = \dfrac{1}{5^\blacksquare}$
 (f) $\dfrac{1}{32} = 3^\blacksquare$

3 Write the reciprocals of the following in the form 2^n.
 (a) 2^5
 (b) 4^2
 (c) 2^0
 (d) 2^{-4}
 (e) 8^2

4 Without using a calculator, write the following as decimals.
 (a) 10^{-1}
 (b) $\dfrac{1}{10^3}$
 (c) 10^{-5}
 (d) 10^{-8}
 (e) 10^{-4}

5 Write the following as decimals correct to 3 significant figures.
   (a) 7^{-1} (b) 6^{-2} (c) $\dfrac{5^2}{3^5}$ (d) 9^{-2} (e) 5×3^{-2}

6 Solve:
   (a) 7^{-1} (b) $5^x = 5$ (c) $4^x = 0.25$ (d) $\dfrac{1}{3^x} = 1$

   (e) $x^{-3} = 0.125$ (f) $10^x = 0.01$ (g) $x^{-4} = \dfrac{1}{81}$ (h) $8^5 = \dfrac{1}{2^x}$

Section F

1 Find the value of n in each statement.
   (a) $2^5 \times 2^{-3} = 2^n$ (b) $7^{-5} \times 7^3 = 7^n$ (c) $3^0 \times 3^4 = 3^n$
   (d) $5^{-2} \times 5^0 = 5^n$ (e) $5^{-2} \times 5^{-3} = 5^n$ (f) $10^{-4} \times 10^{-3} = 10^n$

2 Copy and complete
   (a) $\dfrac{2^3}{2^5} = 2^\blacksquare$ (b) $\dfrac{3^0}{3^5} = 3^\blacksquare$ (c) $\dfrac{5^2}{5^0} = 5^\blacksquare$ (d) $\dfrac{2^{-4}}{2^5} = 2^\blacksquare$

   (e) $\dfrac{3^{-2}}{3^{-5}} = 3^\blacksquare$ (f) $\dfrac{2^3}{2^\blacksquare} = 2^0$ (g) $\dfrac{5^{-2}}{5^\blacksquare} = 5^{-3}$ (h) $\dfrac{7^\blacksquare}{7^6} = 7^3$

3 Write the answer to the following in the form 3^n.
   (a) $(3^0)^3$ (b) $(3^{-2})^3$ (c) $(3^5)^0$ (d) $(3^3)^{-4}$
   (e) $(3^{-2})^{-3}$ (f) $(9^2)^{-3}$ (g) $(27^{-1})^2$ (h) $(9^{-3})^{-2}$

4 Copy and complete these multiplication grids.

(a)
×		5^{-2}	
		5^{-6}	
5^2			5^2
5^{-1}	5^2		

(b)
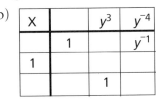

5 Simplify:
   (a) $x^3 \times x^{-5}$ (b) $x^{-2} \times x^{-3}$ (c) $3x^3 \times 5x^{-2}$ (d) $x^2 \times x^{-4} \times x^3$

   (e) $\dfrac{x^5}{x^{-2}}$ (f) $\dfrac{x^{-4}}{x^5}$ (g) $\dfrac{5x^7}{10x^8}$ (h) $\dfrac{x^3 \times x^{-4}}{x^2}$

6 Copy and complete
   (a) $(x^2)^{-3} = x^\blacksquare$ (b) $(x^\blacksquare)^4 = x^{-12}$ (c) $(x^{-2})^0 = x^\blacksquare$
   (d) $(x^\blacksquare)^{-4} = x^0$ (e) $(x^{-5})^\blacksquare = x^{15}$ (f) $(x^{-2})^{-3} = x^\blacksquare$

Mixed questions 1

1 Sadia is carrying out a survey of opinions about school lunches in her class. She gives a questionnaire to all the pupils in the class. Here are some of the questions she asks.

> (a) How often do you have a school lunch? Please tick.   Never ......   Sometimes ......   Always ......
>
> (b) How long do you usually have to wait in the queue?   A short time ......   A long time ......
>
> (c) Do you think that the canteen should offer more vegetarian options, which are more healthy than meat?   Yes ......   No ......

Say whether you think each of these questions is satisfactory. If it is unsatisfactory, suggest a way of improving it.

2 Simplify each of these expressions as far as possible.
(a) $5(x+3) - x(x+1)$ (b) $n(7+n) - 4(n-2)$ (c) $z(4+z) - z(2-z)$
(d) $3k(k-2) - k(k-5)$ (e) $3m(m-1) - m(1-m)$ (f) $4s(5-s) - s(8-s)$

3 Calculate the sides and angles marked with letters.
(a) 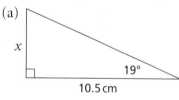   (b) 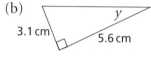   (c)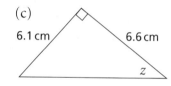

4 Multiply out the brackets and simplify each of these expressions.
(a) $(x-2)(x+8)$ (b) $(y-4)^2$ (c) $(z-3)(z-5)$ (d) $(w+3)^2$

5 Simplify these expressions.
(a) $2a^4 \times 3a^3$ (b) $\dfrac{8a^7}{2a^4}$ (c) $4a^{-2} \times 5a^6$ (d) $2a^2 \times 5a^{-6}$ (e) $(3a^2)^{-3}$

6 This diagram shows the end wall of a shed. Calculate the length marked l.

*****7** Prove that these instructions will always give the answer 6.

> Think of a number (not 0). Add 3. Square the result. Subtract 9.
> Divide by the number you first thought of. Subtract the number you first thought of.

5 Distributions and averages

Section A

1 The number of people in cars that passed a set of traffic lights was recorded. The data recorded is shown in the table below.

Number of people in car	Number of cars
1	10
2	15
3	12
4	6
5	7
6	5

(a) How many cars were surveyed?

(b) How many people were there altogether in the cars?

(c) Calculate the mean number of people per car.

2 The weight of eggs laid by a hen over a period of four weeks is shown in the table. Calculate the mean weight of the eggs.

Weight	58 g	59 g	60 g	61 g	62 g	63 g
Number of eggs	3	7	11	9	8	2

3 Here are the test results for class 10M arranged in a stem and leaf table. Find

(a) The median mark

(b) The range of marks

(c) The modal mark

Marks out of 20

```
0 | 8 8 9 9 9 9
1 | 0 1 1 2 5 5 6 7 8 8 9 9 9
2 | 0 0 0 0 0 0
```

4 (a) Make a stem-and-leaf diagram for this set of examination marks

(b) Find the median mark and the range of the marks

Marks out of 60

19	25	38	48	39	56	42
30	32	39	42	59	28	27
57	45	44	42	37	28	18
55	51	48	36	18	21	24

5 The number of letters delivered to the houses in a particular street is given in the following table. Calculate an estimate of the mean number of letters delivered to each house.

Number of letters	Number of houses
0-3	12
4-7	8
8-11	4
12-15	2

*6 In a darts match a record is kept of the scores for each throw

Score	1-20	21-40	41-60	61-100	101-140	141-180
Frequency	5	20	37	62	6	3

Calculate an estimate of the mean score

Section B

1 The heights of the students in class 10M are measured.

Here are the results

Height (h cm)	Frequency
150 < h ≤ 155	3
155 < h ≤ 160	5
160 < h < 165	7
165 < h < 170	8
170 < h ≤ 175	6
175 < h ≤ 180	1

(a) Draw a frequency polygon for this data

(b) Calculate an estimate of the mean height of the students.

2 For her Geography project Nina collects data about the weekly rainfall (d) in millimetres for her home town. She displays the results in a table.

Calculate an estimate for the mean weekly rainfall.

Weekly rainfall (d) in mm	Number of weeks
0 < d ≤ 10	18
10 < d ≤ 20	20
20 < d ≤ 30	3
30 < d ≤ 40	4
40 < d ≤ 50	3
50 < d ≤ 60	4

Section C

1 The lengths of 36 runner beans were measured and rounded to the nearest mm. Make a frequency table for the given data.
Choose your own class intervals

152 180 165 182 177 160 172 183 163
185 159 176 186 173 189 191 176 192
178 175 173 186 188 193 162 189 168
184 153 170 155 166 184 179 174 171

(a) Draw a frequency chart for the data

(b) From your frequency table, calculate an estimate for the mean length of a runner bean

(c) Calculate the mean of the actual lengths, and compare your estimate with it.

2 The data below shows the amount of rain in millimetres that fell on each day in February

3.5	16.4	6.4	3.7	14.2	8.9	22.9
2.9	7.8	13.9	14.2	4.5	11.6	15.9
18.9	0.1	6.1	1.4	3.1	2.5	5.6
2.6	9.4	4.1	17.9	19.2	10.7	7.2

(a) Draw a frequency chart to show this information.
You will need to choose sensible groups for the data.

(b) Calculate an estimate for the mean rainfall in February

(c) Calculate the mean of the actual rainfall and compare the two results.

Section D

1 The table below shows the quarterly ice-cream sales for a small shop.

Year	1998	1998	1998	1999	1999	1999	1999	2000
Quarter	2	3	4	1	2	3	4	1
Sales	450	850	160	93	380	880	145	86

(a) Calculate a 4-point moving average and show it with the original data on a graph.

(b) Describe the trend.

2 This table shows the amount spent in gas for a family of four.

Year	1998	1998	1998	1999	1999	1999	1999	2000
Quarter	2	3	4	1	2	3	4	1
Amount	£65	£38	£195	£112	£55	£42	£172	£109

(a) Calculate a 4-point moving average and show it, with the original data on a graph.

(b) Describe the trend.

6 Changing the subject 1

Section B

1. This tiling pattern has the formula $g = 2w + 6$.
   (a) Rearrange the formula to make w the subject.
   (b) What is the value of w when $g = 60$?
   (c) What is the value of w when $g = 96$?
   (d) Check that the values of g and w in parts (b) and (c) fit the original formula.

2. Rearrange each of these formulas to make the bold letter the subject.
   (a) $a = 3\mathbf{b} + 7$
   (b) $f = 8\mathbf{g} - 6$
   (c) $r = 12 + 2\mathbf{s}$

3. (a) Make z the subject of the formula $y = 16 - 9z$.
   (b) Find z when $y = 52$
   (c) Find z when $y = {}^-29$

4. Which of the following are correct rearrangements of $t = 6s - 4$.
   (s need not be the subject of the rearrangement.)

   A $\dfrac{t+4}{6} = s$

   B $t = 2(3s - 2)$

   C $t = 3(2s - 2)$

   D $t + s = 5s - 4$

   E $\dfrac{4 - t}{6} = s$

   F $6s - t = 4$

5. (a) Copy and complete this working to make y the subject of the formula $7x - 3y = 50$.
   (b) Use suitable values of x and y to check that your rearrangement is correct.

   $7x - 3y = 50$
   $7x = 50 + $ ❀
   $7x - $ ❀ $= $ ❀
   $y = \dfrac{7x - ❀}{❀}$

6. Rearrange each of these formulas to make the bold letter the subject.
   (a) $a + \mathbf{b} = 14$
   (b) $g = 4 - 2\mathbf{h}$
   (c) $5x + 3\mathbf{y} = 20$
   (d) $p = 2\mathbf{q} - 18$
   (e) $c = 3\mathbf{d} + 7$
   (f) $r = 19 + 3\mathbf{s}$
   (g) $5u = 7\mathbf{v} - 15$
   (h) $8m = 3\mathbf{n} - 15$
   (i) $2d - 3\mathbf{e} = 12$

Section C

1. The formula $s = p + 2r$ connects s, p and r.
   (a) Rearrange the formula to make r the subject.
   (b) What is the value of r when $s = 8$ and $p = 2$?
   (c) Check that this value of r, and the values of s and p fit in the original formula.

2. Copy and complete this working to make h the subject of the formula $j = ah - b$.

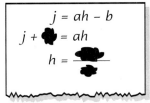

3. Rearrange each of these formulas to make the bold letter the subject.
   (a) $m = k\mathbf{n} + 2$
   (b) $r = m\mathbf{y} - g$
   (c) $b u = 4\mathbf{v} - w$

4. (a) Copy and complete this working to give y in terms of m, x, r and n.
   (b) Use your new formula to find y when $r = 22$, $m = 5$, $x = 2$ and $n = 4$.
   (c) Use the value of y you found in (b) to check that your rearrangement is correct.

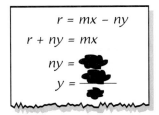

5. Which of these are correct rearrangements of $pn = g - am$?

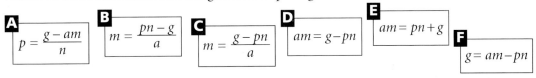

6. A household gas bill is calculated using the formula
   $$C = sd + nu$$
   C is the total cost in **pence**;
   s is the standing charge in pence per day;
   d is the number of days;
   n is the number of units of gas used;
   u is the cost of gas in pence per unit.
   (a) Rearrange the formula to give n in terms of the other variables.
   (b) How many units of gas have been charged for, if the total cost of the bill is £80.94 for a period of 90 days? The standing charge is 10p per day and the cost per unit is 1.1p.

7. Rearrange each of these formulas to make the bold letter the subject.
   (a) $p\mathbf{q} - z = l$
   (b) $f = \mathbf{u} - Ts$
   (c) $h = u + p\mathbf{v}$
   (d) $x_1 = k\mathbf{x_0} - u$
   (e) $am + b\mathbf{n} = 5$
   (f) $2cd + \mathbf{w}v = r$
   (g) $p_1 = sp_2 - g\mathbf{m}$
   (h) $qy = 3a\mathbf{x} - rt$

Section D

1. (a) Copy and complete this working to give s in terms of r and p.

   (b) Find some values of r, p and s that fit the original formula.
   Check that they fit your rearrangement.

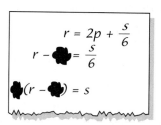

2. Rearrange each of these formulas to make the bold letter the subject.

   (a) $b = 3c + \dfrac{\mathbf{d}}{4}$ (b) $m = 4 + \dfrac{\mathbf{n}}{a}$ (c) $y = 2x - \dfrac{\mathbf{z}}{t}$

3. (a) Copy and complete this working to make t the subject of the formula, where s is the constant speed in m.p.h., d is the distance travelled in miles and t is the time in hours.

   (b) Find the time taken for a car travelling at a constant 56 m.p.h. to travel 266 miles.
   Give your answer in hours and minutes.

4. The volume of a rectangular pyramid is given by $V = \dfrac{abh}{3}$.

   (a) Rearrange the formula to make h the subject.

   (b) Calculate the height of a rectangular pyramid of volume 96 cm³, where $a = 4$ cm and $b = 6$ cm.

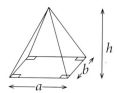

5. Here are 8 formulas.
   Find the four pairs of equivalent formulas.

   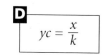

6. The power, in watts, of an electric circuit is given by $W = I^2 R$
   I stands for the current in amps,
   R is the resistance of the circuit in ohms.

   (a) Rearrange the formula to give I in terms of W and R.

   (b) Calculate the current in an electric circuit where $W = 150$ watts and $R = 12.25$ ohms.

7 Make the bold letter the subject of each of these.
   (a) $k = \frac{1}{2}mv^2$ (b) $k = \frac{1}{2}\mathbf{m}v^2$ (c) $M = \frac{pl^2}{12}$ (d) $M = \frac{\mathbf{p}l^2}{12}$

8 Make l the subject of the formula $T = 2\pi\sqrt{\dfrac{l}{g}}$

9 The volume of an Easter egg is given by $V = \dfrac{2\pi r^2 h}{3}$
   r is the radius shown and h is the height, both in cm.

   (a) Rearrange this formula to make r the subject.
   (b) Work out the radius of an Easter egg whose height is 16 cm and volume is 850 cm³.
       Give your answer to an appropriate degree of accuracy.

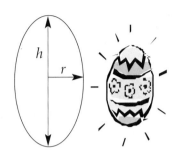

10 Copy and complete this working to make p the subject of this formula.

   Check your rearrangement is correct by substituting values in the original and your rearrangement.

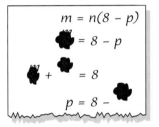

11 Write each formula in terms of the bold letter.
   (a) $c = 16(\mathbf{d} + e)$ (b) $r = m(y - \mathbf{x})$ (c) $j = l + \dfrac{\mathbf{k}}{h}$

12 The extended length of a material with a force applied is given by the formula

   $l = l_0\left(1 + \dfrac{F}{AE}\right)$

   l stands for the extended length in mm
   l_0 stands for the original length in mm
   F stands for the applied force in Newtons (N)
   A stands for the cross sectional area in mm²
   E stands for Young's modulus in N/mm².

   (a) Rearrange the formula to give F in terms of l, l_0, A and E.
   (b) What force needs to be applied to a piece of nylon fishing line of cross sectional area 0.2 mm², to extend its length from 1000 mm to 1005 mm?
       (Young's modulus $E = 2500$ N/mm² for nylon.)

7 Increase and decrease

Section A

1. Write down the decimal equivalent of:
   (a) 46%   (b) 8%   (c) 35.2%   (d) 112%   (e) 7.5%   (f) 137.5%

2. It rained on 13 days during March.
   What percentage of the days in March were rainy?

3. In a box of 24 pencils, 7 need sharpening.
   What percentage (to the nearest 0.1%) of the pencils in the box need sharpening?

4. (a) To increase 85 by 12% you must multiply 85 by ..... ?
   (b) Increase 85 by 12%.

5. (a) To decrease 69 by 71% you multiply 69 by .....?
   (b) Decrease 69 by 71%

6. (a) Increase £125 by 18%   (b) Decrease £150 by 22%

7. A shop reduces prices by 12% in a sale.
   What is the sale price of a coat costing £135?

8. A firm is going to give its workers a 5% pay rise.
   What will be the new rate of pay of a worker earning £8.60 per hour?

9. A car costing £15 000 when new was sold for £11 400 when it was one year old.
   What was the percentage decrease in value?

10. Two years ago a house was worth £150 000.
    During the first year its value increased by 8%.
    During the second year its value decreased by 1%.
    What is its value now?

11. A 330 ml can of drink costs 52p.
    The can is to be replaced by a 500 ml can costing 69p. Calculate
    (a) the percentage increase in the size
    (b) the percentage increase in the cost
    (c) the percentage change in the cost per litre

Section B

1 This diagram represents a 10% increase followed by another 10% increase.

(a) Calculate the overall percentage change.

Calculate the overall percentage changes represented by these diagrams:

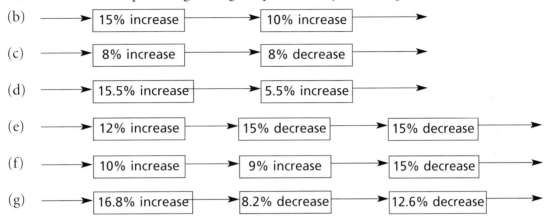

2 A firm gave its workers a 4% pay rise last year and a 3.8% pay rise this year.

Calculate the percentage pay rise over the two years to the nearest 0.1%.

3 Over the past three years, the volume of water in a pond has decreased by 10% each year.
What is the overall percentage decrease over the three years?

4 In January a garage reduced the price of a car by 8%.

In February the garage reduced the price of the car by a further 7%.
What was the overall percentage decrease in price?

5 Last year a travel agent increased the price of a holiday to Spain by 8%.

This year they decreased the price by 5%.
What was the overall percentage increase in price?

6 The population of a town decreased by 3.8% in 1996.

The population increased by 3% in 1997.
What was the overall percentage change in population?

7 Over two years the average attendance at a football ground increased by 26%.

The attendance increased by 15% in the first year.
What was the percentage increase during the second year?

Section C

1. £650 is put into a bank account which pays interest at the rate of 8% per annum.

   Copy and complete this table showing the amount in the account at the end of each year.
   (round to the nearest penny)

Years	Amount
0	£650.00
1	£702.00
2	
3	
4	

2. Stephen invested £700 in a building society account that was paying 4.5% p.a. interest. How much did he have in his account after:

   (a) 1 year   (b) 2 years   (c) 3 years   (d) 4 years

   (round your answers to the nearest penny)

3. Which is larger, the final amount if:

   (a) £500 is invested for 3 years at 4% p.a.   or
   (b) £500 is invested for 4 years at 3% p.a.?

4. Calculate the final amount, to the nearest penny, when:

   (a) £750 is invested at 5% p.a. for 8 years
   (b) £850 is invested at 3.75% p.a. for 12 years

5. £2000 is invested in an account which pays interest at 6% per annum.

   How many years will it have to stay in the account before it is worth £3000?

6. The value of a painting increases by 4% each year.

   If it is worth £350 now, how much will it be worth in 10 years time?

7. The number of people attending a cinema decreases by 6% every year.

   What is the overall percentage decrease in attendances over 3 years?

8. A bank charges interest on a loan at a rate of 1.8% per month.

   Calculate the overall percentage rate per year giving your answer to the nearest 0.1%

9. Samantha opens a new bank account with £1000
   She pays an extra £1000 into the account at the end of each year.

   How much will there be in Samantha's account when:

   (a) her first extra payment is due
   (b) her second extra payment is due
   (c) her fourth extra payment is due?

Section D

1. The population of a town increased by 5% during the last ten years.
   The present population is 16 000.
   What was the population ten year ago? (Round your answer to the nearest 100.)

2. A television costs £399.
   This price includes VAT at 17.5%.
   What is the cost of the television before the VAT is added?

3. A shop reduced the price of shoes by 25% in a sale.
   A pair of shoes cost £24 in the sale.
   What was the price of the shoes before it was reduced for the sale?

4. A restaurant includes a service charge of 12% which is added to the bill.
   A customer in the restaurant paid £19.60, including service charge, for a meal.
   What was the price of the meal before the service charge was added?

5. The cost of a drawing program was reduced by 10% to £89.99.
   What was the cost of the software before the reduction?

6. The price of a radio was increased by 5%.
   If the new price of the radio is £38, what was the increase in price?

7. The number of viewers watching a weekly television programme increased by 15% when an episode showed the two stars getting married.
   5.4 million watched the wedding episode.
   How many more people watched the wedding episode than the episode the previous week? (Give your answer correct to 3 significant figures.)

8. A dress which should have been dry cleaned shrank by 6% when it was washed by mistake.
   The length of the dress after it had shrunk was 105 cm.
   How many centimetres did the dress shrink?

9. A magazine's sales figures have dropped by 12% in the past year to 32 478.
   How many more copies did the magazine sell last year?

Section E

1. The number of squirrels in a wood has increased from 242 to 248 in the past year.
   (a) Calculate the percentage increase in the number of squirrels.
   (b) If the number of squirrels continues to increase at the same rate each year, how many squirrels will there be in the wood in 5 years time?

2. A garage owner reduced the selling price of a car from £6299 to £5999.
   (a) What was the percentage reduction in price?
   He still could not sell the car so he reduced its price by a further 7.5%
   (b) What was the final selling price (to the nearest £)?
   (c) Calculate the overall percentage decrease in price.

3. The owners of a toll bridge increase the toll for cars crossing the bridge by 8%.
   As a consequence, 5% of the drivers who used the bridge decided to use an alternative route. Calculate the percentage change in toll money taken.

4. John increased the area of his lawn by 11% to 204 m².
   What was the original area of the lawn?

5. April 1998 was a particularly wet month with 124.9 mm of rain falling on average across the UK.
   This rainfall was 102% higher than the normal average rainfall for April.
   (a) What is the normal average rainfall for April across the UK?
   (b) How much more rain than normal fell in April 1998?

6. £3200 was invested in a new bank account 5 years ago.
   Each year, interest has been added at the same rate.
   The account now contains £4084.10
   Calculate the rate of interest.

Mixed questions 2

1. Rearrange each of these formulas to make the bold letter the subject.
   (a) $b = 4(\mathbf{a} - 1)$
   (b) $q = \dfrac{3\mathbf{p} - 1}{2}$
   (c) $d = 5 - 3\mathbf{c}$
   (d) $t = 8 + \dfrac{\mathbf{s}}{2}$

2. The population of a town is planned to increase by 15% over the next three years and by 10% over the three years after that.

   The present population is 24 600. Calculate, to the nearest hundred, the planned population in six years time.

3. This table shows the distribution of the weights of some young children.

   Calculate an estimate of the mean weight of the children.

Weight, w kg	Frequency
$3.0 < w \leq 3.5$	8
$3.5 < w \leq 4.0$	14
$4.0 < w \leq 4.5$	11
$4.5 < w \leq 5.0$	7

4. Calculate the length CD in this diagram.

5. The value of a house drops by 7% in the first six months of the year and then increases by 12% in the second six months.

   Calculate the overall percentage change over the whole year, to the nearest 0.1%.

6. Re-arrange each of these formulas to make the bold letter the subject.
   (a) $y = a\mathbf{x}^2 + b$
   (a) $y = ax - \mathbf{b}$
   (b) $w = \dfrac{\sqrt{\mathbf{u} - st}}{n}$
   (d) $t = p + \dfrac{q\mathbf{s}^2}{r}$

7. Marji opens a building society account with £200.
   The building society pays interest at a rate of 5.5% a year.

   How many full years will Marji have to leave the money in the account for it to grow to at least £250?

8. Calculate the length QR in this diagram.

   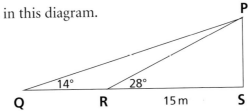

8 Sine and cosine

Section A

1 Find the missing angles and lengths.

(a) 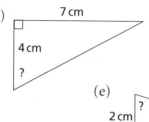 (b) 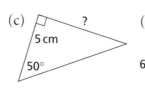 (c) 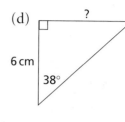 (d)

(e)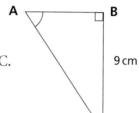

2 In a triangle ABC, tan A = 0.25.
   (a) What is the length of AB?
   (b) Using Pythagoras find the length AC.

3 Find the missing lengths.

(a) 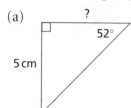 (b) 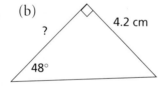 (c) (d)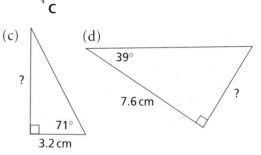

Sections B, C and D

1 Find the missing angles in these right-angled triangles.

(a) (b) 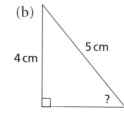 (c)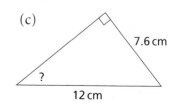

(d) 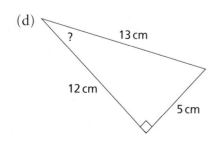 (e)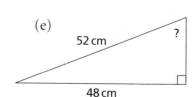

2 Find the missing lengths.

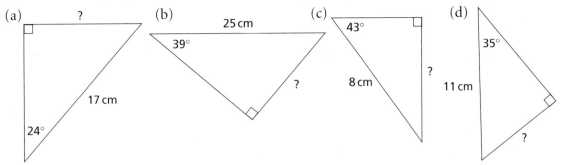

3 Find the missing lengths

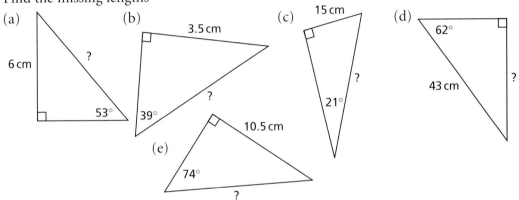

Section E

1 Copy and complete these diagrams and statements.

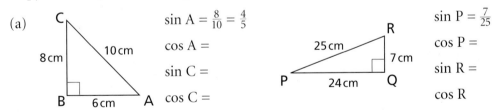

(a) $\sin A = \frac{8}{10} = \frac{4}{5}$

$\cos A =$

$\sin C =$

$\cos C =$

$\sin P = \frac{7}{25}$

$\cos P =$

$\sin R =$

$\cos R$

2 Find the missing angles.

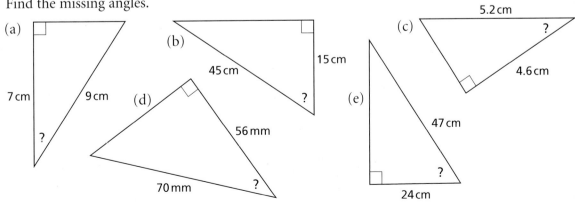

3 (a) If $\cos A = \frac{3}{4}$, what is the angle A? (b) If $\cos A = 0.5$, what is angle A?

4 Find the missing lengths in these right-angled triangles.

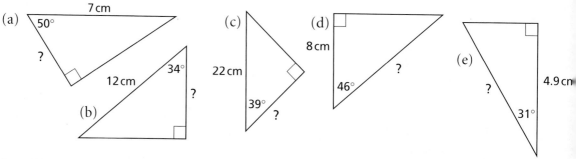

Section F

1 Find the angles or lengths marked x in each triangle.

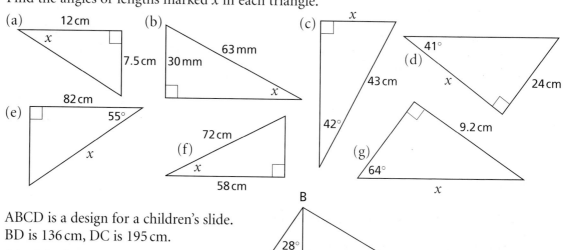

2 ABCD is a design for a children's slide. BD is 136 cm, DC is 195 cm.

(a) Calculate angle BCD.

(b) Angle ABD is 28°. Calculate the distance AB.

3 The angle of elevation of a kite is shown from 2 positions, Q and R. PQ = 70 m.

(a) Calculate the height of the kite PS.

(b) Calculate the length RS.

4 The height of a yacht's mast BE is 8 m. Calculate length AD.

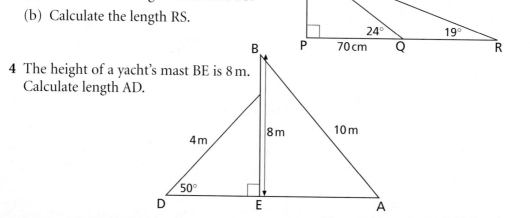

9 Using area and volume

Sections A and B

1 Calculate the areas of these parallelograms.

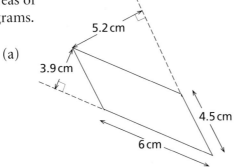
(a)

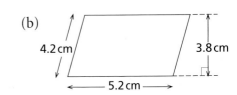
(b)

2 Find the missing lengths in each of these parallelograms.

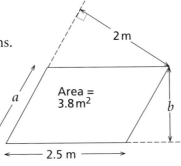

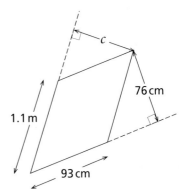

3 The area of each of these three parallelograms is 76.8 cm². Find the missing lengths.

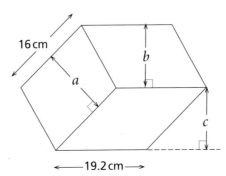

4 These triangles have equal areas. Find the missing lengths.

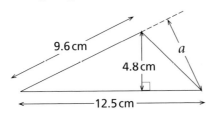

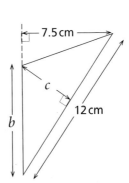

5 Find the shaded areas.

(a)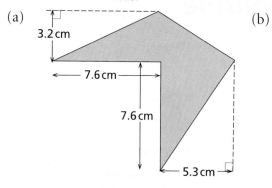

(b)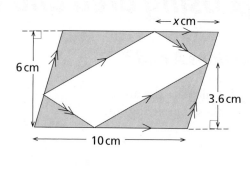

*****6** Find the total shaded area.

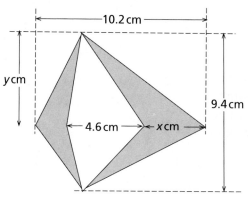

Section C

1 Find the area of these trapeziums in (i) mm² (ii) cm².

(a)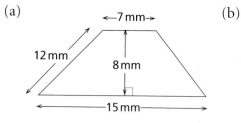

(b)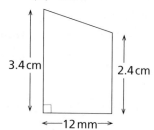

2 Find the missing lengths in these trapeziums

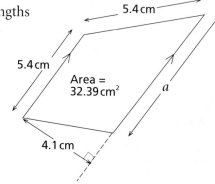

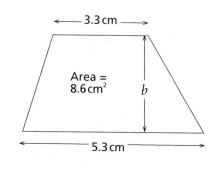

3 This graph shows part of the curve $y = x^2$.

Use triangles and trapeziums to work out an estimate for the area under the curve from $x = {}^-2$ to $x = 4$

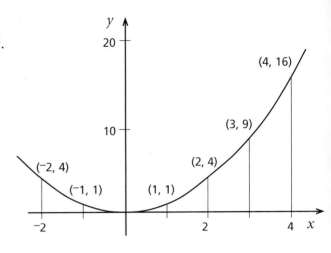

Section D

1. This table shows typical yields from some vegetables.
   (a) What weight of potatoes should you get from a plot with area $20.5\,\text{m}^2$?
   (b) What weight of broad beads should you get from a rectangular plot $4.2\,\text{m}$ by $1.5\,\text{m}$?
   (c) How many cucumbers should you get from a rectangular plot $2.5\,\text{m}$ by $0.5\,\text{m}$?

Vegetable	Yield
Aubergine	$5.0\,\text{kg/m}^2$
Broad bean	$3.8\,\text{kg/m}^2$
French bean	$2.5\,\text{kg/m}^2$
Cucumber	16 cucumbers
Potato	$4.0\,\text{kg/m}^2$

   (d) What area is needed to get 22 kg of broad beans (to the nearest $0.1\,\text{m}^2$)?
   (e) A gardener has a plot with area $6.5\,\text{m}^2$.
   He wants to fill it, growing aubergines and French beans only.
   He wants the weight of French beans he grows to be twice the weight of aubergines.
   What area should he give to each crop and what weights would he expect to get?

Section E

1. (a) How many cubic metres of water are needed to fill this swimming pool?
   (b) The inside of the pool is covered with white tiles.
   Calculate the approximate number of tiles needed if each tile measures 20 cm by 20 cm.

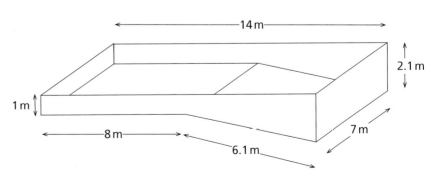

Section F

1. A set of ten cork table mats each measuring 31.5 cm by 20 cm by 4 mm has a mass of 0.605 kg.

   What is the density of cork?

2. The density of sugar is 1.59 g/cm³.

   What is the volume of a kilogram bag of sugar?

3. This picture shows an aluminium-framed greenhouse which is delivered as a kit including all the glass.

   The glass is 3mm thick horticutural grade glass with a density of 2.4 g/cm³.

   What is the mass of the glass? (ignore space taken up by the aluminium frame)

   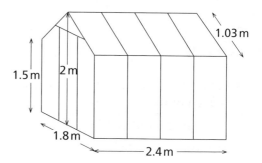

4. An open box consisting of four sides and a base is made of mahogany with a thickness of 12 mm.

   (a) The density of mahogany is 0.85 g/cm³.
   What is the mass of the box?

   (b) A box of the same dimensions is made of pine 19 mm thick.
   This box has a mass of 5.06 kg.
   What is the density of the pine?

   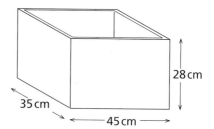

Section G

1. A table cloth measures 150 cm by 240 cm.
   (a) Calculate the area of the cloth in cm².
   (b) Convert your answer to m².

2. A piece of paper measures 0.6 m by 0.45 m.
   (a) Calculate the area of the paper in m².
   (b) Convert your answer to cm².

3. A credit card measures 8.5 cm by 5.4 cm.
   (a) Calculate the area of the card in cm².
   (b) Convert your answer to mm².

4. A bucket can be filled with 12 000 cm³ of sand.

   How many buckets of sand can you get from 1 cubic metre of sand?

10 Large and little

Sections A and B

1 A car owner drives an average of 20 miles every day.
   At this rate, how many years would it take him to drive a million miles?

2 A quadrillion is 10^{15}.
   Write this number out in full.

3 Iceland has an area of 103 000 sq km.
   Which of the following are ways to write its area?
   (a) 103 thousand sq km (b) 1.03×10^5 sq km (c) 10.3×1000 sq km
   (d) 103×1000 sq km (e) $1.03 \times 10\,000$ sq km (f) 10.3×10^3 sq km

4 If you take 13 cards at random from a shuffled pack of playing cards, the chance that they are all the same suit (e.g. all clubs) is approximately 1 in 1.6×10^{11}.
   How many billion is 1.6×10^{11}?

5 Satellite data and ground rainfall measurements were used to study variations in the size of the Sahara Desert from 1980 to 1997. The area of the Sahara Desert varied from 9 980 000 km² in 1984 to 8 600 000 km² in 1994 and had an average area of 9 150 000 km².
   (a) (i) Write the maximum, minimum and average areas of the Sahara desert between 1980 and 1997 in millions of km².
       (ii) What is the difference between the maximum and minimum area?
   (b) About 5×10^7 km² of the Earth's land surface is desert.
       How many million km² are desert?

6 The table shows the areas of the seven largest oceans and seas.
   (a) Copy the table writing the areas in millions to the nearest million km².
   (b) The total area of sea is about 360 million km².
       What percentage of the sea is taken up by the Pacific Ocean?

Pacific Ocean	166 242 000 km²
Atlantic Ocean	86 557 000 km²
Indian Ocea	73 427 500 km²
Arctic Ocean	13 224 000 km²
South China Sea	2 975 000 km²
Caribbean Sea	2 516 000 km²
Mediterranean Sea	2 510 000 km²

Section C

Do not use a calculator for this section.

1. Write these numbers in standard form
   - (a) 4 000 000
   - (b) 28 000
   - (c) 603 000
   - (d) 10 000 000
   - (e) 416 000
   - (f) 32 000 000 000

2. Write these numbers in ordinary form
   - (a) 3×10^5
   - (b) 1×10^8
   - (c) 3.2×10^4
   - (d) 6.3×10^3
   - (e) 2.86×10^4
   - (f) 6.13×10^9

3. Write these numbers in standard form
   - (a) 35×10^3
   - (b) 627×10^4
   - (c) 300×10^5
   - (d) 0.8×10^4

4. Between 1947 and 1980, 450 000 people died in earthquakes.

   Write the number of people who died in earthquakes in standard form.

5. The table shows the attendance figures for the first six years of the Premier Football League (to the nearest 100 000)

   (a) Rewrite the table giving the attendances in standard form.

Year	Attendance
1992-3	9 800 000
1993-4	10 600 000
1994-5	11 200 000
1995-6	10 500 000
1996-7	10 800 000
1997-8	11 100 000

   In 1998–9, the total attendance figures for the Premier League and the Divisions 1 to 3 was 25.4 million people

   (b) Write this number in standard form.

6. The circumference of the earth is approximately 4×10^7 m.

   Write this distance as an ordinary number.

   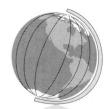

7. The average distance of the moon from the earth is 3.844×10^5 km.

   Write this as in ordinary form.

Section D

Use a calculator for this section.

The information shows the population (1999) and the area of different countries.

Country	Population	Area (sq km)
Brazil	2.7×10^8	8.4×10^6
China	1.3×10^9	9.9×10^6
India	1.0×10^9	3.1×10^6
Russia	1.5×10^8	1.7×10^7
South Africa	4.3×10^7	1.2×10^6
United Kingdom	5.9×10^7	2.4×10^5
United States	2.7×10^8	9.1×10^6

1 (a) Which of these countries has the smallest area?

　(b) Does the largest country have the largest population?
　　　Explain your answer.

　(c) Does the smallest country have the smallest population?
　　　Explain your answer.

2 Copy and complete the following statements.

　(a) The area of China is about .... times the area South Africa.

　(b) .... more people live in Brazil than Russia.

　(c) The area of the United States is about .... times the area of the United Kingdom.

　(d) The population of India is about .... times the population of Brazil.

　(e) China is .... sq km bigger than India.

　(f) Russia is .... sq km bigger than the United States.

3 The population density of a country is the number of people who live in each square kilometre.

$$\text{population density} = \frac{\text{population}}{\text{area}}$$

　(a) Calculate the population densities of each of the seven countries, giving your answers correct to 1 significant figure.

　(b) Arrange the countries in order of population density, highest first.

Section E

Do not use a calculator for this section.

1. Write these numbers in ordinary form
   (a) 1×10^{-2}
   (b) 2.3×10^{-4}
   (c) 3.8×10^{-6}
   (d) 5.1×10^{-4}
   (e) 2.6×10^{-12}
   (f) 8.08×10^{-7}

2. Write these numbers in standard form
   (a) 0.000 003
   (b) 0.000 006 72
   (c) 0.000 569
   (d) 0.000 000 001
   (e) 0.000 300 8
   (f) 0.000 000 000 000 4

3. If you take four cards from a pack of playing cards, the probability that they are all aces is 0.000 003 69. (correct to three s.f.)
   (a) Which of these are ways of writing this probability?
      (i) 36.9×10^{-5}
      (ii) 3690×10^{-9}
      (iii) 369×10^{-4}
      (iv) 36.9×10^{-7}
      (v) 369×10^{-8}
      (vi) 0.369×10^{-5}
   (b) Write the probability in standard form.

4. A nanosecond is 0.000 000 001 seconds.
   Write this number in standard form.

5. A scruple was an old measure used by apothecaries.
   One scruple weighed about 1.3×10^{-4} kg.
   Write this number in ordinary form.

6. The probability of rolling six consecutive sixes when rolling a standard dice six times is 2.14×10^{-5} (correct to three s.f.)
   Write this probability in ordinary form.

7. A honeybee uses up 8×10^{-4} Joules of energy for every wingbeat.
   Work out how much energy is used for 50 wingbeats and write the answer in
   (a) standard form
   (b) ordinary form.

8. The lightest recorded insect is a parasitic wasp which weighs 5×10^{-9} kg.
   Write this weight in ordinary form.

Section F

Use a calculator for this section.

1 Write the answer to these calculations to two significant figures in standard form.
  (a) $(4.8 \times 10^{-6}) \times (4.6 \times 10^{-7})$
  (b) $(1.6 \times 10^{-4}) \times (3.8 \times 10^{3})$
  (c) $\dfrac{6.7 \times 10^{-6}}{5.7 \times 10^{7}}$
  (d) $\dfrac{8 \times 10^{3}}{1.03 \times 10^{-5}}$

2 Write the answer to these calculations in ordinary form giving your answers correct to two significant figures.
  (a) $(3.6 \times 10^{-2}) \times (5.2 \times 10^{3})$
  (b) $(5.1 \times 10^{6}) \times (3.9 \times 10^{-7})$
  (c) $\dfrac{1.2 \times 10^{6}}{3.0 \times 10^{-7}}$
  (d) $\dfrac{7.2 \times 10^{-4}}{9.8 \times 10^{-4}}$

3 An amu (atomic mass unit) is 1.66033×10^{-27} kg.

  What will be the mass in kilograms of a particle with mass 15 amu?

The table shows the atomic mass of various elements measured in amus

Element	Atomic mass (amus)
Lead	207.19
Oxygen	15.9994
Copper	63.546
Zinc	65.381
Sulphur	32.064
Hydrogen	1.0079

4 Copy and complete these statements, giving your answers correct to three s.f.
  (a) The mass of an atom of lead is $207.19 \times (1.66033 \times 10^{-27})$ kg $\approx$ .... kg
  (b) The mass of an atom of copper is about .... kg
  (c) An atom of zinc weighs about .... kg more than an atom of copper.

5 A molecule of water consists of two atoms of hydrogen and one atom of oxygen.
  What is the mass, in kg, of one molecule of water? (correct to six s.f.)

6 A molecule of copper sulphate consists of one atom of copper, one atom of sulphur and four atoms of oxygen.
  What is the mass, in kg, of one molecule of copper sulphate? (correct to six s.f.)

Section G

Do not use a calculator for this section.

In questions 1 to 3, give your answers to the calculations in standard form

1. (a) $36 \times 10\,000$ (b) $0.29 \times 100\,000$ (c) 53×10^6
   (d) 0.03×10^7 (e) 71×10^{-3} (f) 0.29×10^{-4}

2. (a) $78 \div 1000$ (b) $106 \div 1\,000\,000$ (c) $5.9 \div 10^6$
   (d) $7.2 \div 10^{-8}$ (e) $0.38 \div 10^{-7}$ (f) $0.03 \div 10^9$

3. (a) $\dfrac{64000000}{8000}$ (b) $\dfrac{1.2 \times 10^{11}}{3000}$ (c) $\dfrac{2.4 \times 10^8}{6 \times 10^5}$
   (d) $\dfrac{9 \times 10^4}{3 \times 10^{-6}}$ (e) $\dfrac{4.5 \times 10^{-7}}{9 \times 10^3}$ (f) $\dfrac{6 \times 10^{-5}}{1.2 \times 10^3}$

4. Calculate the following giving your answers in ordinary form
   (a) $(3 \times 10^3) \times 10^5$ (b) $(2 \times 10^{-4}) \times (6 \times 10^5)$ (c) $(7 \times 10^{-9}) \times (3 \times 10^4)$
   (d) $\dfrac{3.6 \times 10^3}{10^5}$ (e) $\dfrac{4.8 \times 10^4}{1.2 \times 10^2}$ (f) $\dfrac{6 \times 10^{-5}}{1.2 \times 10^3}$

5. (a) Round each of these numbers to 1 significant figure.

   $A = 2.36 \times 10^8$ $B = 2.89 \times 10^{-7}$

   $C = 4.7 \times 10^{-3}$ $D = 6.45 \times 10^{10}$

   (b) Use your answers to work out an estimate for each of these calculations. Give your answer in standard form correct to 1 significant figure.
   (i) $A \times B$ (ii) $B \times D$ (iii) $B \times C$
   (iv) $D \div A$ (v) $B \div D$ (vi) $C \div A$

11 Gradients and equations

Sections A and B

1 Find the gradient of each of these lines.

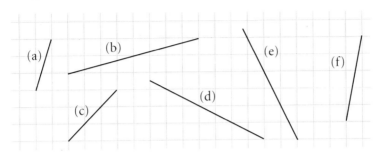

2 On squared paper draw lines with gradients
   (a) 2   (b) ⁻3   (c) 0.5   (d) –1

3 Find the gradients of the lines joining
   (a) (0, 2) and (2, 4)   (b) (⁻1, ⁻4) and (2, 5)
   (c) (⁻2, 0) and (2, ⁻4)   (d) (⁻4, 1) and (4, ⁻3)

4 Roger walks from Vendrell to the beach at Salvador and then returns to Vendrell. The travel graph of his journey is shown. For each stage of the journey describe fully including times taken and speeds.

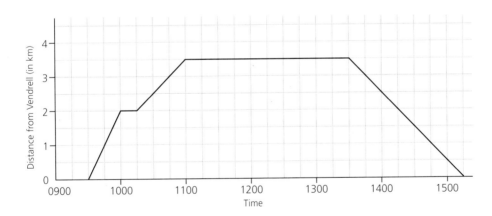

41

Sections C and D

1. For each line in the diagram on the right,
   (i) What is the gradient of the line
   (ii) Where does the line cross the y-axis?
   (iii) Write down its equation

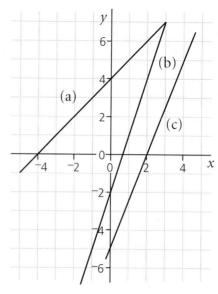

2. A line has equation $y = 5x + 3$.
   From the equation write down the gradient of the line and where it crosses the y-axis.

3. A line has a gradient of $^-2$ and crosses the y-axis at (0, 4). Write down the equation of the line.

4. A line has a gradient of 7 and passes through the point (0, 0). Write down the equation of the line.

5. A line passes through the points (0, 4) and (6, 4).
   (a) What is the gradient of the line?
   (b) Write down the equation of the line.

6. A line passes through the points (0, 6) and (6, 0).
   (a) What is the gradient of the line?
   (b) Write down the equation of the line.

7. A line has equation $y = ax + b$.
   (a) What is the gradient of the line?
   (b) What are the coordinates of where it crosses the y-axis?

8. Write down the equations of any three lines that are parallel to
   (a) $y = 2x - 6$
   (b) $y = ^-x + 5$

9. Calculate the gradient of each line using the scales on the axes.

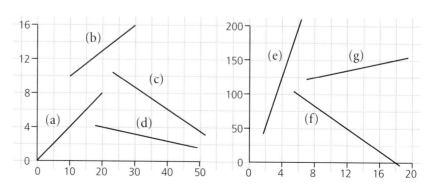

10 For each of these grids
   (a) find the gradient of each line
   (b) find the equation of each line

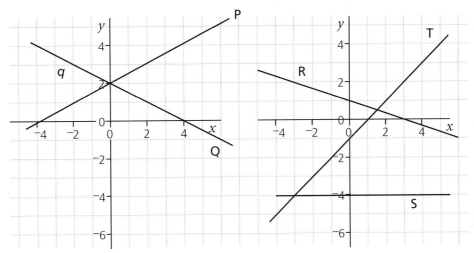

11 A line has a gradient of $\frac{2}{5}$ and it cuts the y-axis at (0, 4).
   Write down the equation of the line.

12 A line has equation $y = \frac{3}{4}x - 2$.
   (a) What is the gradient of the line?
   (b) What are the coordinates of the y-intercept?
   (c) The line passes through the point (4, 1).
       Find another pair of integer coordinates that the line passes through.

13 A line has equation $2y = x + 4$. It passes through the point (2, 3).
   (a) Find another point the line passes through.
   (b) Find the gradient of the line.
   (c) Find another way of writing down the equation of the line.

Sections E and F

1. On squared paper draw lines with gradient
   (a) 1 (b) 2 (c) $\frac{3}{2}$ (d) $\frac{-1}{4}$
   Draw the lines perpendicular to each one above and label it with its gradient.

2. A line has gradient $\frac{4}{5}$.
   What is the gradient of the line perpendicular to it?

3. A line has gradient $\frac{p}{q}$. What is the gradient of the line perpendicular to it?

4. What is the equation of the line perpendicular to $y = 2x + 4$ and that goes through $(0, ^-2)$?

5. Find the gradient and y-intercept of lines with the following equations.
   (a) $^-3x + y = 5$ (b) $5 - x + y = 0$
   (c) $3y + 10x = 3$ (d) $4x = 2(3 - y)$

6. Write the down the equations of any three lines parallel to
   (a) $2x - 2y - 7 = 0$ (b) $2x - 3 + 4y = 0$

7. Which of the following equations represent lines that are perpendicular to each other?

   | $2y = 2x + 10$ | $2y = ^-x + 5$ | $2y - 3x = 6$ |
   | $2x - 15 - 3y = 0$ | $x + y = 5$ | $2x - y = 0$ |

8. Shape PQRS is a kite.
   ∠PQR = 90°.
   The line through QR has equation $2y + x = 4$.

   Find the equations of lines through PQ, PS and RS.

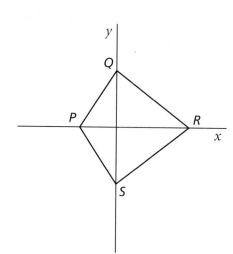

Section G

1. Find, in the form, $y = mx + c$, the equation of
   (a) the line through (4, 70) and (7, 82)
   (b) the line through (27.8, 14.4) and (28.3, 13.4)
   (c) the line through (5, 2) and (13, 4)
   (d) the line through (−21, 6) and (14, −1)

2. The shape *PQRS* is a square.
   The coordinates of three vertices are
   P (14, −10) *Q* (20, 20) and *R* (50, 14).
   Find the equations of the lines through *QR*, *PQ* and *RS*.

3. The lines $y = rx + 4$ and $3y = (r + 3)x - 5$ are parallel.
   Find the value of *r*.

4. Television repair charges depend on the length of time taken for a repair.
   Here are some of the charges.

Time in minutes (*T*)	50	80	100	180
Charge in £ (*C*)	35	50	60	100

   (a) Draw a sketch graph of the time (*T*) against the charge (*C*).
   (b) Find the equation that links the charge and the time in the form *C* =
   (c) What is the fixed amount for a repair – sometimes known as the "Call-out Charge"?
   (d) Use your equation to work out the charge for a repair that takes $3\frac{1}{2}$ hours.

Section H

1 Sue dropped a bouncy ball from different heights. She measured the height of the first bounce each time. Here are her results.

Height ball dropped from (in cm)	30	50	80	100	120
Height of first bounce (in cm)	15	32	52	70	81

   (a) Plot the points and draw a line of best fit. Estimate its gradient and y-intercept to one significant figure. Hence find an approximate equation for your line of best fit.

   (b) Use your equation to estimate how high the ball would bounce if dropped from a height of

   (i) 65 cm

   (ii) 2 m

2 Jo wants to buy a new car. She collects information about engine capacity and fuel economy (the number of miles per gallon). Here are her findings.

Engine capacity in litres	1.1	1.3	1.6	1.8	2.3	3
Fuel economy (mpg)	45	41	37	34	28	22

   (a) Plot the findings on a graph and draw a line of best fit.

   (b) Find an approximate equation for the line of best fit.

   (c) Estimate the fuel economy of a car with an engine capacity of

   (i) 2.1 litres

   (ii) 3.5 litres.

   Which of your estimates will be more reliable?

   (d) Jo wants to buy a car with fuel economy of 50 mpg. What engine capacity should she consider?

Mixed questions 3

1. Calculate the sides and angles marked with letters.

   (a) 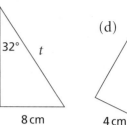   (b)   (c) 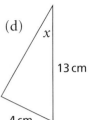   (d)

2. Find the equation of:
   (a) the line parallel to $y = 5x - 3$ going through $(0, 2)$
   (b) the line parallel to $x + 2y = 5$ going through $(0, {}^-4)$
   (c) the line perpendicular to $y = x + 3$, going through $(1, 1)$

3. Do these without using a calculator.
   (a) Write 0.000 001 42 in standard form.
   (b) Work out $(4 \times 10^7) \times (3 \times 10^{-3})$, giving the result in standard form.
   (c) Work out $\dfrac{2 \times 10^{-2}}{4 \times 10^4}$, giving the result in standard form.

4. Which of these statements are identities?
   A $n(n - 1) = n^2 - n$
   B $(n + 3)(n - 4) = n^2 - 7n - 12$
   C $(n + 1)^2 = n^2 + 1$
   D $(n - 1)(n - 5) = n^2 - 6n + 5$

5. How many litres of water will this skip contain when it is full?

   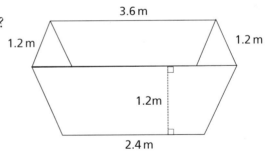

6. Calculate the angle ABC in this diagram.

   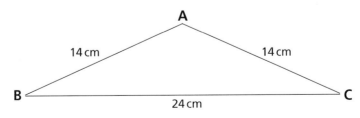

7 Find the value of n in each of these equations

(a) $5^3 \times 5^n = 5^6$
(b) $2^n \times 2^5 = 2$
(c) $7^2 \times 7^n = 7^{-2}$
(d) $\dfrac{3^3}{3^n} = 3^5$

8 ABCD is a kite.
The diagonals AC and BD cross at E.
AB and AD are each of length 5 cm.
BC and CD are each of length 7 cm.
Angle BAD = 128°.
Calculate

(a) BD
(b) angle BCD

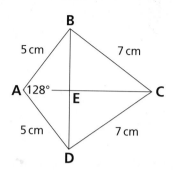

9 ABCD is a rectangle.
Find

(a) the gradient of DC
(b) the equation of AB
(c) the equation of BC
(d) the equation of BD

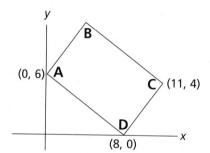

10 Multiply out the brackets on both sides of each of these equations and solve the equations.

(a) $(x + 4)(x + 3) = (x + 1)(x + 9)$
(b) $(x + 5)(x - 2) = (x - 3)(x + 8)$
(c) $(x - 3)(x - 6) = (x - 4)(x + 3)$

11 Work these out without using a calculator.
Give each answer in standard form.

(a) $4 \times 10^5 + 2 \times 10^3$
(b) $4 \times 10^5 \times 2 \times 10^3$
(c) $4 \times 10^5 - 2 \times 10^3$
(d) $\dfrac{4 \times 10^5}{2 \times 10^3}$
(e) $\dfrac{1}{4 \times 10^5}$
(f) $\dfrac{2 \times 10^3}{4 \times 10^5}$